After Ward

After Ward

Poems by Wendell Hawken

Cherry Grove Collections

Published by Cherry Grove Collections
P.O. Box 541106
Cincinnati, OH 45254-1106

ISBN: 9781625494115

Poetry Editor: Kevin Walzer
Business Editor: Lori Jareo

Visit us on the web at www.cherry-grove.com

Cover art by Pam Bernard
"Homage to de Kooning," ink and acrylic on vellum

Do not babble in the assembly of the elders
And do not repeat yourself when you pray.
                              Ecclesiasticus 7:14

For Freddie and all the clients and staff at **Ability Fitness Center** in admiration of their grit and courage. And for his sister Ashley and the KA's of UVA, his steadfast brothers.

Table of Contents

Reader

Hopper, Edward. *Hotel Room.* 1931, Museo
Nacional Thyssen-Bornemisza, Madrid.

A woman in a peach slip—
remember slips?—sitting on the bed's edge

reads a piece of paper held like a tray:
thumbs on top, fingers underneath.

A note of apology?
The docent says *train schedule.*

I am old enough to know,
yes, they looked like that.

The hotel room a spare but complicated
space—a Hopper, after all.

Absorbed by what she reads,
the woman –*Jo, his wife,* again that docent—

sits framed within a frame. Her day clothes
laid with care across the chair,

suitcase and valise unopened where
she set them down,

the yellow window shade three-quarters
pulled against the flat black night.

Kicked-off heels her one untidy moment
as she undressed, sat to read.

Collision

West of Beckley on the West Virginia turnpike
where the road climbs and swerves
the Blue Ridge, where crumpled guardrails
evidence laws of trajectory, weight and speed,
peripheral movement in an upland pasture
becomes, at full glance, a yearling deer
running flat-out and angled toward the road.
I check my mirrors for future lane change
possibilities as the deer, and now another
behind it deeper in the field, close the distance
to our future up ahead.
                          Another look: the first
deer leaps, flings itself at high-tensile fence
but breasts the wire, somersaulting to collapse,
legs churning a faint recall of run
while what I had seen as a second deer
lifts it head, softening its gait to lope in
on the downed one: a coyote—
huge, bushy-coated, sharp-nosed coyote.
I swear, it seems to smile as I hurtle past
and all my mirrors fill with mountain
and trees, tender green with new leaves.

New Time

If it all comes true, every bit of it,
every tarot card, queen of clubs, every lightning
bug that ever trudged a life-line
to the high point of a hand,

if space bends, as they say, and gravity is
up for grabs, its force perhaps too strong,
too weak, or as just right as Baby Bear's chair,

if our skies hold history
and every star shine comes from past time
to meet the present eye,
it is possible to wish the wish you wished
tonight on an extinguished star
which may or may not
matter for the wish.

Likewise, if the absence of evidence is,
as they also say, evidence itself
and you had the choice,
even had to choose
the falling back to old time
having tired of the new,
the Ouija answers every question
Yes! and the chicken livers look
propitious in the pot
being boiled for the dogs.

If you walk out in a sunrise, orange rising into white,

dogs will leave you to the gravel two-track
having beasts to tree or send to ground
and though you might not see them,
they will you, moving past the grazing cattle
who raise their heads and deem you harmless.
You can watch them think it
as they stand and stare and chew.

Following Cloven Meander

Dew-white webs
soon to disappear in
warming.

The pile of
a small meat-eater's
blood-black scat.

White belly hairs
on fence wire's
barbed stars,

and tufts
in mashed shit-stained
grass

tell the night's tale
I do not mind
not knowing.

Beware

The rehabilitation process typically begins in the acute care setting.

Locked doors open with a bleating bell
(rhymes with *fell*).

So, beware, you walking ones, coming two
by two on assumed feet,

breathing unassisted breaths,
too pink, too tan, too altogether

colorful for this cool gray overhead florescence
where the weather's off-white 68 degrees

and time hangs black-rimmed on the wall,
round with pulsing hands—*his cannot move*—

a place where everything's on wheels—
the golf cart rolled three times

before it pinned him in the pond—
you who clutch your helpless Mylar and helium,

who hand out soft treats
so the attending ones in white might come

sometimes when you say *please*
when you call *help*.

The bitter cup burns your lips, words
never dreamed of knowing, filled overflowing.

You walkers, walk the pale linoleum,
the only path on which the non-anointed

may tread (rhymes with *dread*)
come to hold

unfeeling hands, speak softly
to the face not too bruised and swollen

not to be
beloved beneath the swelling.

Beware, you who lack badge or bracelet,
those looping tentacles and tubes

measure, measure,
chart and measure

the flowing in and out, graphing
patterns sharp and round.

How shrill their sudden cries:
the language of this cool pale place,

the sibilants that matter.
And here you thought—*foolish woman*—

you had gotten past the need
to keep him hidden

from sharp yellow teeth
and hungry tongues. Here you thought

you left that horror
back there in the half-grown woods.

       **

Which is why
walk is not a word

to use, not when anyone
might hear.

Whisper, if you must
invoke the god

of useful limbs,
limbs obedient

as he was as a child
though you should know

before you ask:
in ancient times

the household gods were
always hardest to appease.

I'm just saying.

TICU

GUSTO GUSTO:
Told it's code
for his drugs first

in the intensive
days they also say
he will not

remember when
he reclaims
his given

name, with
GUSTO GUSTO's
gone.

Acute Care Setting in the Traumatic ICU

Exodus 3:1-15

Beyond wilderness
at the mountain of god
remove your sandals

bare your feet on holy ground
flame of fire from the bush
unconsumed and blazing

hear the whisper from the bush
all ate the spiritual food
all wondered at the rock not a rock

believe in the whisper
reading the psalm
to the son in his bed in the TICU

the psalm his friend sent
in the letter he wrote
reading psalm's words

at one side of his bed
his nurse joining in, reciting
by heart,

my broken first-born
surrounded by testament
surrounded by words

words wafting and rising
the curtain pulled round
holding words in

in the TICU
at the mountain of god
and there for the first time,

the only thus far,
the hover of Presence
wrapping us there

benign and a comfort
air thickened with words
as we chanted the psalm,

Nurse Sheila and I,
in the terrible time
of the trach and the tubes,

the suction of mucus,
counting of calories,
the new words to learn,

all the pillows to prop,
and the tubes,
so many tubes.

Dream of Riding a Difficult Horse

As salt or sugar leaves
taste to water,
the dream's vague residue
hints a saddle-bag
and curb-bit dream
astride a hard-mouthed ride
skirting edges
of the wakened mind
blinded by bright day,
itself a dream of being.

Naked on the Pond Dock Under Night Sky

Tick tock the mindfulness clock
harkens deep in star-flecked dark
Rorschached with moon's ragged edge
verging on an opening mind —
wind and weather not withstanding—

and in that vast outlasting place
space surrounds the midnight words:
Lord have mercy fall on specks at sea,
maybe those on rafts, and maybe me.

Tick tock the luminous clock
interlocks with moonless dark,
clicks the seconds into quarter hours
scouring the day's dirt edge
dredging silt, thoughts left behind
to find an understanding.
Hands curled at his breast
suggest bird feet clutching branches
and here the rush of time and place
interface where rote words
afford relief from after-shock.

If This Is

If this is not the line   there is no line
there is no telling   if this cannot be told

no weeping telling

if this is not the question   there is no question
no flowers heaped   no candles lit
            no messages on walls.

If this is not the limit   if this is not the edge
there is no   where else to fall

resting foreheads   against a cool stone wall.

If this is   how it is
how close the future is   to coming

if this is not the end   after such beginning
there is no end   in sight

if this is just   the hiss
            before the bite.

Break Neck

The American Spinal Injury Association (ASIA)
Impairment Scale: A – E

ASIA-A is
most profound.

ASIA, not the continent,
the acronym.

For some weeks
we thought *ASIA-B,*

B meaning some function
below the C4.

C for Cervical
meaning neck.

There are seven Cs,
twenty-four articulating

vertebrae in all,
T for the twelve

Thoracic,
L1-5 for Lumbar.

C1-3 cannot breathe
without machines.

There's that.

Plus his intact mind.

Evenings, the day nurse
summarizes for the night

standing at his bed
recites name, age, *ASIA-A*.

Twice a day: *ASIA-A*.
Profound, its second meaning.

Not deeply knowledgeable,
its first.

ASIA-E means walking
to the mailbox,

means bringing back
the mail, one-handed.

E means everything
before.

That he can feel his toes,
hypodermics in his thigh

does not mean
what we believed.

Frontal nerves are motor;
the back ones, sensory.

We did not know

that then.

We thought anything
meant everything.

In Silence Wrapped

Wrapped in a dark cloak
cloaking sight, the ears
hear rodents rustle moonstruck.

A struck-numb sun lifts
drifts of dark cloth. The farmer
farms grass pasture, plowing silt

built by swollen overflow—
how the river gifts downstream
slipstream against a backstroke oar.

Hear the white words until
chilled limbs go numb
from cold-burn ever

closer to the time all become
numb-struck under withdrawn sun
one word and world away undone.

Night at Shepherd Center

Following a spinal cord injury, the individual's respiratory muscles become weak and, in turn, the patient is unable to cough. This results in the accumulation of secretions within the lungs.

A *Shepherd Night*
means hard to breathe,

means respiratory techs
red-button responding,

the whine and beat
of wheeled-in suction machine,

a flat-hand press on diaphragm
to cough assist. *Good one*

means green mucus moving
down the suction tube.

Doing great. Now push again,
push harder.

You can't hurt him.

Status

*Over 80% of the spinal injuries reported occurred
in males.*

A guy named Cornflake
two rooms down.

Hey, Corn, my son nods as he powers by,
right hand on the throttle.

How ya doin, answers Corn
who flat-lined five times,

has two good arms,
a manual chair with transfer

board in the chair's back pocket
sticking up like status.

To Be

...with very few patients experiencing any
substantial recovery more than nine months after
the injury.

In the land of *If* during days of *When*
there is the hand-held horror
of forever.

In a land of bare flat floors,
smooth as any doctor's answer
where there are levers, never

knobs or thresholds,
most every patient's male,
every door wheelchair wide.

At a button's wail comes
the *slap, slap* of soft shoes
on linoleum

as the days of *When*
diminish, the verb *to be*
becomes more common

in often simple, positive
sentences of a static state
but connective, a linking

to show existence
or condition

often used with others,

though highly irregular
(in conjugation,
not in meaning)

and some manuals say weak,
without style
and advise to eliminate

to be from one's writing
so there is
no is at all.

Dream of Centrifuge

In the part of night that's morning
to waken in the dream again—

not the late dream with no ticket,
the sweet one: worth it, no matter what,

where wind sounds like far-off water,
random white seeds floating past

as minutes blown in dandelion time
lying on the soft damp grasses

living in a land of deep belief
planets spinning in the centrifuge of I,

to waken to the tilt and shift
lying on the lush damp grasses

hearing ripe plums summon honeybees
humming their warm continuum

in a land of spread-out peace,
wind-sound like water in the leaves

in the dream that brings relief.

Hope is the Word for Despair

If hope is a cold porridge sister
who sits on her stool,
sings to herself a nonsense tune,
over and over
the same three notes
while the beside-her spider
hums along
as best a *noiseless patient* spider can,
hope is also a line
through the dust on the sill;
an irregular verb in the future tense.
Hope is tense in the present,
always looking ahead.
If hope is a hard-mouthed horse,
a little hot but not
so hot not to ride (a good ride too
once the edge wears off),
hope is a cat high in an elm,
backing down.
If hope is a martini mother,
hope is also the olive
left in the glass.
Hope is the un-emptied glass.
Also winter grass ruffling
before it clarifies
as not the cat crossing the pasture
padding home.
If hope is no longer the testimonies,
each day a page with recovery's story,

page after page flying away,
hope is the guy who got back his arm,
the use of an arm
after one year of not moving,
returning like the cat thought lost
same as always at the door.
Hope is her small red bowl on the floor.

Cath

*A suprapubic catheter is inserted in the bladder through a
small hole in the belly.*

Small clots too
will be passing
down the tube

surgically inserted.
Pink's okay.
Red's the worry.

Or clots
too large to easily
pinch free.

Half a year:
how we watched
as widows pacing parapets,

his body our horizon.
At first, we welcomed
spasms.

Enough times told,
the what-happened words
distance into story.

We now say *cath*
for catheter as if speaking
of a close friend.

There are the growing
gestures of his arms: shake,
salute, you name it.

Family Dinner

His eyes resting on the purple
sunken half-moons of his day

he feeds himself with his specially
bent fork inserted in

his hand's black brace. His wife moves
close behind his wheelchair,

lays her arm across his chest.
His stronger right arm lifts to stroke hers.

He shifts his head to touch her shoulder,
shuts his eyes. She rests her cheek

against his head, her eyes focused on a future
far from here,

the Wolf Moon at the window,
shining in.

At the Kitchen Window

The seeded feeder swaying peaceful for the most part,
peaceful but for the hammer-headed jays.

Who can name a scene that lacks—implied
or otherwise—its hammer-headed jays?

To wander the *what-if* landscape
under dark of threatened rain,

swollen knuckles aching,
night slides out the way he left:

imperceptible until it's not.
Do you have to hit every pothole?

Never mind the scold-bird, no matter its insistence
within the thorny branches of the honey locust tree,

its cry may be a mere transference.
Settle yourself into a feet-up peace before the stirrings:

dogs' deep rhythmic breathing, click of ceiling fans.
All teaspoons, it is true, but spilling in abundance.

Somewhere out there may be found the kindness of a cat,
way out beyond the birds.

The great upheaval is beneath us, bare white
given way to prime dandelion time,

the brevity of bluebells,
old adversaries of pokeweed, wild onion picking up

where they left off as if they had never been away
which, of course, they hadn't.

Poem

Here's the thing: a poem needs a bird,
words with wings and thus some sky
high blue and wildly yonder.

Another thing: a poem needs necessity
gritty past mere compression, a *raison*
woken by sound in time

to strum, tapping feet to mind-music
trafficking brain's both sides
riding sound to recognition,

no plot or arc, but music as its meaning:
sing of pollen and bloom
summoning the hum of honeybees.

See how a poem needs its bees.
Needs its hum and birdish words
to nudge narrative into being.

Feeling's the thing. In certain times
rhymes stay pithed and pinned,
thin as winter harvest, a feeder absent seed.

Walking Down the Farm Lane to Retrieve the Morning Paper

After a dreaming thin ice night,
the scrub woods stark and flat
as a woodcut illustration
comes a cat-lap morning
through summer whitewash of Marguerites,
Queen Ann's Lace.
  Untrimmed fruit trees
yield scant fruit. What fruit there is
sways out of reach
though one recent season, peaches
hung in earth-bound plenitude
so heavy the boughs broke.
  Mid-field,
pungent waft of fox. Hounds could hunt
if today's a hunting day.
This is the season.
  A red-tail hawk, the smaller male,
prey lassoed in his talons—black snake,
probably. Hard to tell from here
as his wings work across a watercolor sky,
itself a revelation after wild rain.
The old dog in the house, done in by thunder.
Air hangs water-thick.
Leaves turn light-side out.
Branches tremble as another dark disturbance
threatens to roll in.
  At the county road,

the hiss of bamboo canes enlarges
its percussive. A white-muzzled red fox
bursts in view, ears back at its pursuer –
though, in truth, not seeming all that worried,
loping across the asphalt and away.
      Out of the same thicket
comes the neighbor's dog, plants front feet
in roadside surveillance—a piece of Kabuki,
well-rehearsed.
I pick up the paper with its day-old news
that's new enough.
      Some days, ants are
small dark ants, not floaters in the eyes.

Can Live

Without the falling
leaves, without evening
swallows braiding purple sunsets.

Don't need the hum of insect legs
to recall good sex.

I have my pines
to occupy the kitchen panes
and hang my feeders on,

to gather close where I can see
wrens, sparrows,

chickadees, to hear
chirping praise of birdseed
generosity.

Close, I hang my feeders close.

Hands

Sling lifts are used for patients whose mobility is limited.

Gone, too,
golf calluses,
his thinned fingers
seem longer now.

Fingers of a pianist
or painter.

Still life in a sling
as an engine hoisted
from a car frame.

Look, he says and lifts
his weaker left hand

in a loose-wrist
gesture of *No more,*
stop

or *Comme ci,*
comme ca.

How he would call
for me to come

watch boyhood's bike
zoom down the driveway,
legs out wing-like,

both hands
off the handlebars,

laughter trailing out
behind him
like a tail.

Gravity

Try it sometime.
Try flinging
an arm up using
biceps,
just your biceps,
(if you can
isolate them)
to feel the work
it took to learn
to lift (fling)
his forearm up
against gravity
to feed himself
if someone puts
a plastic fork
(metal too heavy)
between his teeth
so he can bend down
and push its handle
in his right-hand brace
to jab the food
put on the plate
set on his lap.
His neck now
weight-lifter thick
between his sloping
shoulders.
Did you know
a quadriplegic's arm

bones can detach
spontaneously
from shoulder joints,
and internal organs
shift around?

Side by Side

To live on the other side of silence
where the squirrel's heart
drums the sparrow's wingbeat,
where whitetails metronomically
bound away. Even the bucks.
Especially the bucks,
high-headed bucks burdened by horn.

To yearn in a place where words
are breeding birds back from mystery
ready to mate, where farm gates
swing open into White Oak groves,
the domestic turned out to graze
with the wild, side by side,
not to dwell but abide.

To reside in a place where the red
thread of forgiveness weaves
a running stitch through the soft cloth
of these times, hemming raveled
sleeves of men. Especially men,
knife-wielding men dressed in black,
explosives strapped to belly and back.

To lack hands-up answers to the unasked
where violence tastes like food, to crave
the rusty tang of blood, where lost thoughts
lie with the slow work of hope,
a single cello's downbow resounding

over rubble of a bombed-out city square
in a place not far from here.

Dream with Doubt

A farm lane long and straight,
not a winding-over-rock outcrops
like the farm lane here.
So the place is not this place.

A fellow gets dropped off,
swaddled in a blanket.
                              Smaller than
he was, no bigger than a toddler,
one bandaged nub protruding
from his pelvis like a tail.

The dream before he had
two nubs, was altogether larger
though his head full-sized
unchanged.
                    He smiles to say, *Just fine*—
a sweet smile like my son's—
but in the dream I doubt it.

Microcosm in Rain

I'll give her a year.
               -the father-in-law prophesied

After the third-grade performance
in sudden, though predicted, rain,
the robed Joseph and his brother
belted in the van, I maneuver
wheelchair ramp, straps, and locks
to bolt my son their father in.

Across the lot comes their mother
who, in truth, might have made
a gesture or suggestion before
she steps back, chirps, *See ya,*
and fades—no, more like flounces—
to disappear inside the downpour.

Bed-Rest Day

On the wide screen TV
Duke is playing
Clemson for the ACC.

Pressure wounds will
tunnel to bone.
And have.

His wound photos could be
worst-case textbook
illustrations.

At first, I thought
his bedside's blackish-
yellow tube to be

his catheter.
Are you stoned?
Yes, he nods.

His son's emoji pillow
props his head,
protein shake

pressed between braced hands:
a marionette
with slackened strings.

At the half,

Duke is leading
by two foul shots

taken at the buzzer.
Anything can happen.
There's still time.

Willful Movement. Some Function.

A stem cell study in New Jersey is
going on right now.

Epidural stimulation in Kentucky
reports willful movement of the legs.

I don't care if I look like Frankenstein.

His C-4 has biceps only, as you know,
and he can fling his right forearm

to raise his braced hand to his face.
If someone puts plastic fork tines

between his teeth he can slide the handle
into his brace, lift the lightweight plastic,

feed himself. You know that too.
I like to re-tell all his doings.

The San Diego monkeys
got *'some forelimb function'* back

and by now the Swiss mice
in their mice-sized harnesses

must have been replaced
by monkeys, if not yet humans.

I wonder how much the *'some'*
in *'forelimb function'* is.

Sorry, mice.
Sorry, monkeys.

Sorry all you creatures out there
with your severed spines.

I find you hard to think about.

But to see him on the bed-rest days
to ease his pressure wounds:

Biafra-thin,
white top sheet an almost-shroud,

his Adam's apple
the largest thing about him.

> *Days like this can crack you in half.*

Strange but in his power chair, khaki pants,
starched collared shirt and glasses,

I almost forget him otherwise.

Creed, Nave, Science Fair

Needlepoint for kneeling, organ music
fills the belly up—it's Bach—crashes off
cathedral's stone canopy, ribs enough
to sit me insignificant as quick

and dead. I sit and stand to mouth out those
ought not confessions. Not quite penitent
enough, well knowing what the warnings meant,
I study stone. Light through stained glass bruises

church stone. Does the organ also stain stone—
could chords be cast off color after light
to nameless hues across nave stone—or might
notes become cloud or color, either one?

I sit and find myself preferring what
I cannot bring vague thoughts to reach around—
this grasp and slip of light on stone. And sound.
How winter breath will wisp the same for mute

as sound, the time I watched a display screen
as pixel points of similarity
changed the tiger's face to Shasta daisy
to walnut tree—here, there—I have seen

one flow from the other as easily
as mood. The pixels grasp and slip each change
as summer nimbus clouds rearrange
the sky. I have seen daisies come from trees.

I've watched my metamorphosis to me,
seen light-on-dark of my own x-rayed bone,
how light casts stained-glass stories onto stone
whose ends come absent any guarantee.

On Finding a Snakeskin

Envy the snake
its fit of new skin,
time and again
as long as it lives
growing longer
and rounder
perpetually greater.
Envy its leaving
all constriction
behind, most silent
of creatures evolving
itself by unhinging
its mouth.

Newspaper Photograph

The angled photograph reveals
the crown of her head, face obscured,

ruffled red bodice, smooth red silk skirt,
shapely café-au-lait calves and ankles

tapered into five-inch (at least) stiletto heels.
Red, of course, and matching.

She could have been—and was— any woman
laid out in ruffled red (which is not to say

there was ever more than one Aretha)
all doodled up (my mother's voice)

but here's the thing: they had her legs
crossed at the ankles, left over right,

as if kicked-back relaxing post-performance
and in a way you could say she was.

As I double-knot my Nikes

I flash to the time when I cannot,
as my son will, most likely, never—
absent *deus ex machina*.
There's that.

Six years in, I heard he gave them
all away. His shoes, that is.

Did you see the Tom Hanks movie – not
"Extremely Loud and Incredibly Close,"
but the one in which he also dies,
then returns to watch his family?
Tom Hanks, I think it was.

Last Saturday at youth soccer, my son
inside his custom van,
the solid curb impassable.
Plus what jostle does to pressure wounds.
How hot it was.

We sat in the cool closed space
watching from a distance his two sons
run and block the ball and kick.

Her new husband is their coach.
She struts the sideline in a floppy straw hat
I recognize from before.

In her tank T, her still-taut ass in skinny pants,

she does look fetching.

He is so thin, my son.

Did you know, before they drink or graze
in a new pasture, cattle will plod
fence lines of their turn-out
gauging the boundary of their being
in the place in which they find
themselves delivered?

Dream as Told to Me

Waves come in.
Her brother lies on shore.
Where his wheelchair—how
he got there?—it is a dream.
She holds his head up: my daughter
with her brother. The tide keeps
coming in. Her brother's head
gets harder, heavier to hold,
water rising, rising until her brother,
himself the father of two boys,
tells his sister, *Enough.*
Just let me go.

VR

Same old story.
Same word order.

Reciting
the what-happened

unchanged
as my son.

He dreams he walks.
Has begun a beard,

chest-strapped upright
in his power chair.

His red trach mark
lightened white.

All these years in,
I hold out

an envelope
for him to take.

Secular Psalm

If you could see dawn's white whisper
turn an unmown field and random trees
into a Turner landscape of muted
color and light, you might feel better
about being in the world:
in the sweet of staying put,
in the daily exercise of dogs,
in—now a mother's voice—*routine.*
I had my time, she also said.
But only once.
And near the end.
Perhaps you also dream your mother
floating with you in a boat,
a beautiful pea-green boat.
Better for a necessity of meaning.
It seems a waste for the unnecessary
to occupy the pages of a life,
especially as pages fill and plot
reveals itself. Or not.
Myself, I have come to crave
compassion in my readings:
humane protagonists who love the world.
Or try to. To crave a word-dream
not too much in the culture
I am out of, dream as tonic to the real.
To see as peaceful (when I know they're not)
these pastures off the front porch,
once shrouded white.
I wish you could see this place,

and hold it in your mind: morning mist
dissolving as warm wind does its sway
and leaf-dance with the trees
now in the school of maybe Constable.

Dream on the Accident's Anniversary

I am to take him to the doctor.
A two o'clock appointment.
We are in my girlhood home.

Driving uptown almost to the District line
I notice he is not inside the car.
It is my car, not his van, he is not in.

I speed back, navigate barricades
not there before, dash into the house.
The kitchen clock, both hands up,

reads ten of two and there he is:
no wheelchair, standing at the sink,
fixing food for his two boys.

The linoleum floor is thick with dust.
I begin to vacuum up the clumps.
An unknown boy comes in, *Who are you?*

Driving Dream

Late summer of the mind
when green has gotten as far
and wide as green will spread
and climb, days of warm and groggy
napping, here comes
the driving-blind dream
recurring as my mother had her
house dream: two wings—one full of life,
the other empty.

-What happened?
-Nothing, it just stopped.

In my driving dream, sight comes
and goes. I must force my eyelids open.
Often, I cannot.
Driving by feel and intermittent sight,
I miss the turn,
continue to a fork,
slide into a round-bale barricade
midways in the road,
round bales not of rolled-up hay
but patchwork quilts.

Hunger

A pair of Red-tails write, re-write
wing-spanned cursives.

How safe rhyme feels,
huddled in its burrow,

how unexpected it can turn
in search of sound:

when beauty needs no sleep
and snow's no longer white

all the princes in the land
turn soft as anthracite

as morning's walk with dogs
eases present into past—

Wordsworth walked for rhythm
or was it Coleridge?—

The old dog, not unlike the mind,
comes when good and ready,

not when called.
If at all.

A treat bag helps.
Did you know plastic bags are banned

in Tanzania?
I saw a sheltered workshop

making totes with glue, newspaper,
knotted twine for handles.

His CB handle: Apple Man.
Copacetic a word he used,

meaning hunky-dory,
though nothing he would've said:

hunky dory. Hunky meant Hungarian
in my mother's Carbon County, PA

childhood near the mines
where she was a Mick.

Her best friend Magda, a Rusky,
went to the Steel Pier in Atlantic City

to ride the horse off the tower
into a tiny pool.

In Cuba, I saw the writing tower
Hemingway never wrote in,

the one his wife had built.
The row of dog headstones.

An accordion-sided stray,
front paws on a pizza box

as he rips and swallows
greasy cardboard.

Or the guide telling of Cuba's
"Special Period,"

the marinated cloth
tied to a string, he would chew

and swallow, bring back up
to marinate and eat again.

Flea Market Exchanges

Bought an eggplant
for its heft and shape,
shiny purple slick, almost slimy skin,
calyx remnants curl-tipped
as a jester's hat.
          Thought about
three tennis balls for a dollar.
          Watched the bird lady
fold cardboard into a box,
jab holes into its sides,
thrust her practiced hand
into a pet carrier—suddenly
cheeping—retract her fisted catch
to jam into the fresh-made box.
          Just like that.
Two dollars.
The girl has four.
I say, *The chick needs a friend*.
The boy beside her in shoes too-big
says, *Gramma said one*.
          They walk off,
box cradled in her arms.
          The chick might live.
In my version, the chick does live
a long and happy life.
It is a lucky little chicken.
Girl and chicken love each other
into ever after

as the picture fades to blank screen
and a slanted white cursive scripts *The End.*

Trail Ride through Katherine's

A small skull at my horse's feet,
sunken flat, tufts of gray on bone,
open jaw, long curved canines,
leg bones tucked.
Something died here.
The others circle horses:
What—half-grown coyote—gray fox?
My grandson, one rider says
turning back onto the trail,
would collect the bits,
take them home,
boil them,
then put the whole thing
back together.
        In a white-limbed
sycamore, crows mob a perched red-tail.
My little horse breasts his way
through a tangle of storm-felled oak,
jigs afterwards in celebration.
I let him.
        Back to business,
he climbs a rain-gouged wash
into a stun of yellow coreopsis,
ten planted acres, maybe more,
all blooming mass and dazzle
bordered by a strip of tall thin grass,
strangely blue,
mowed paths on which to ride
as if we were expected here.

Something is expected.
There is a ladder to a tree stand.
A great blue heron rises loose-winged
from pond shallows. One kingfisher
skips its surface like a well-thrown stone.
Belly up on the bank, a silver canoe.
My little horse, surrounded by bee murmur,
ambles through the lure of coreopsis bloom
and seed-head dream,
headed home.

Revolver

1.
After the coywolf came
after my dog and me
and drove us from the far field,

I bought a 38,
empty first chamber
just in case.

There is, per se,
no safety.

2.
Whatever
killed the black cat
killed him in the barn aisle,

blood and black tufts
where he sunned
warm afternoons, where
he fought back.

The brindle ran off
or got eaten
elsewhere.

Rooted

Not the refrigerator
humming food's abundance,
(wonderful as it is)

not the cat lapping
fresh well water—
another wonder—from her bowl,

that is, the cat's a wonder
but the water's more,

not the fuck-me
frenzy of spring birdcall
out there *carrying on* (a mother's voice)

I have learned to say:
listen to your heart's beat
and beating at breath's door,

in the rhythm of yourself
and know yourself alive in a day
all yours to squander,

your own precious daylight
to burn a hole in (a father's words).
You have made

the bed you lie in,
the one the dog jumped down from,

that you slid out of,

smack dab into a sentence-ending
preposition that flouts the old rules
in the small red book.

You leave the grammar
lost as you hustle into over-sweet
pungency of locust bloom,

sweeter than lilac,
than Wild Olive,
locust blooms profuse

in this holding spring,
its old-fashioned linger, reminding
how springs used to be,

how your memory says they were.
Everywhere, trees pull that same
green trick from their brown sleeves,

a trick to sort the living
from the dead.
        You mourn your hundred

towering wild Ash trees,
groves you did not notice
until they died, now skeletal

and broken in the rock outcrops
flanking the house.
        You did not hear them

scream when emerald ash borers
struck so fast the trees lacked time
to defend against the burrowed

hieroglyphic chewing on their trunks—
artful markings
but for the consequence.

Art has consequence.
        Once a Southern Catalpa
I lived beside, a specimen of a tree,

had a caterpillar horde,
come feasting on its palmate leaves,
so many caterpillars

their barrel-shaped shit sounded—
I kid you not—
like rain on the tin roof.

The Catalpa must have called
the swarming tiny wasps
whose planted eggs

quilled caterpillar backs—fat white quills—
whose pupae ate the caterpillars
inside out.

        They weakened in slow motion,
the caterpillars—I cheered their falling—
in time to leave leaves enough

to save the tree, a somewhat rare
but truthful ending for the tree,
the wasps and summer shade.

Such a caterpillar horde, some few
must have made it past the wasps
into caterpillar rapture.

Now What?

pressure sores are the first risk factor with immobility…
infections can lead to death

No more *quadriplegia,*
language

having moved to *tetraplegia.*
The Greek more chic.

We say quad, say spasms.
Not dyskinesia, Not spastic hypertonia,

his feet strapped
to wheelchair footpads

too tight
(*tightly,* murmurs my corrector,

the one inside beside my mother)
but no, better

the spit out fricative of a *tight*
than the softening suffix

to explain the pressure sore
we call wound in his right foot.

Sore not enough.
A splinter's sore.

Or perhaps caused
not by constriction.

Perhaps he broke
a toe, going feet first

as he must,
a break not felt

for lack of feeling,
his pinky crying

whee-whee-whee
all the way home

as infection
burrowed to bone.

And the next
had none.

Both all gone, plus partial
metatarsals.

His foot, he says,
looks like a sloth's.

I saw the video.
It does.

A large black X
marks the spot

where the piggy
having none

and the crying one
had been.

Longer

In the longer version of my life
I will see cures for cancers.
Understand dark matter.
From our blue marble Goldilocks
answer Fermi's Paradox.

In the longer version of my life
gravity will be explained.
I will understand the workings
of the human brain.
Where this need for conflict dwells.

In the longer version of my life,
the summer cold is just that.
No need to clean out closets.
Write down passcodes.
Find a future for the dogs.

I would have liked to walk with him
through the poems of his life
if not hand in hand, then parallel
smell his smell, hip to hip
my days overlapping his.

I would have liked to try
his glasses on my eyes, see his take
on future times, witness the persons who
my grand-kids grow into, would have liked
this breeze to be his hands ruffling my hair.

Ten Years In

At the edge
of understanding I asked
if he had given up.
No, but it's hard.
So hard sometimes.
You have no idea.

I walk the farm, parallel
the neighbor's woods
wild with habitat.
Every kind of thorny scrub.
Where coyotes come from.
Some nights fill back fields
with their high-pitched
hunger songs.
Shudder for the dogs and me
safe inside,
for remnant legs, always the legs
the dogs will find,
tall grass crushed by struggle.
He knows he can be dismissive,
sharp. Says all-night spasms
give him *a low reserve.*

I walk to walk the helpless off,
get my per diem in.
What lies past
wood's edge in *dark and deep:*
more thorn and fallen limbs,

       old oaks larger-seeming
fallen, lying every which way
like a gigantic game of pick-up sticks
       where the stick you lift
cannot move another stick
or you loose your turn.
       He's right.
I have no idea.

Notes

May 7, 2011. The first Saturday in May. Kentucky Derby. The phone call a parent dreads. Then Atlanta's Shepherd Center and the tumble down the rabbit hole of disability with Freddie's quadriplegia. These poems calmed my helplessness and I hope they might offer others the comfort of shared experience.

As Freddie adapted, the critical need for exercise and the lack of local facilities in Northern Virginia became clear. Five years of fundraising, and a partnership with The Arc of Loudoun (VA) created **Ability Fitness Center**, a non-profit special needs gym for members with physical or neurological challenges. Led by its Clinical Director Helen Parker, **Ability Fitness Center** changes lives, workout by workout. It's where the magic happens. Google us.

"Hope is the Word for Despair": the phrase *noiseless patient* from the Walt Whitman poem "A Noiseless Patient Spider."

"Ten Years In": the phrase *dark and deep* from Robert Frost's "Stopping by Woods on a Snowy Evening".

Acknowledgements:

"Gravity" and "Poem" won their respective 2019 Poetry Society of Virginia annual contests.

"Newspaper Photograph" appeared in the *Adelaide Literary Review*.

The following seven poems appeared in the chapbook *The Spinal Sequence* (Finishing Line Press, 2013):

"Collision", "Beware", "Break Neck", "At the Shepherd Center", "Hope is the Word for Despair", "Hands" and "Cath".

Thanks to Kevin Walzer and Lori Jareo of Cherry Grove Collections who believed in this work and to my Warren Wilson friends and colleagues who offered support and wise critique including Don Colburn and J.C. Todd of Wally Camp manuscript review, Marie Pavlicek-Wehrli, Susan Sindall, Mary-Sherman Willis, and Pat Corbus.

Wendell Hawken came to poetry late in life and earned her MFA in Poetry at Warren Wilson decades after college. Her publications include three chapbooks and three full collections: *The Luck of Being* (2008), *White Bird* (2017) a sequence about her husband's battle with cancer, and *Stride for Stride: A Country Life* (2020).

Hawken lives on a grass farm in the northern Shenandoah Valley where the weather means more than what clothes to wear, and the first meaning of AI is Artificial Insemination. Two dogs keep her company.

Made in USA - Kendallville, IN
40670_9781625494115
07 08 2022 1340